MAGICAL RITUALS FOR

LOVE

BY DONNA ROSE

Visit us on the Web:
www.OCCULT1.com

ORIGINAL PUBLICATIONS
NEW YORK

MAGICAL RITUALS FOR LOVE
© 2006 by ORIGINAL PUBLICATIONS

ISBN: 0-942272-81-1

Original Publications
P.O. Box 236
Old Bethpage, New York 11804-0236
1-888-OCCULT-1

TABLE OF CONTENTS

A Message for you ....

This is a book of easy-to-do Spells for Love, and the rituals you can use to help you obtain your goals in Love.

You have the ability to control your thoughts and to use them to help fulfill your life. With determined concentration and positive thought, Seals, Talismans, Stones, Candles and Incense all release magical powers creating favorable conditions for your desires to be obtained. Chanted words ensouled with mental visualization and empowered by the strong desire spread a sonic vibration outwardly into the ether and cause an echo affect upon the "Astral" levels of the emotional feeling and project to the subject of your desire.

Belief is the main key to making not only the rituals you will find in this book work, but to making all magic work. Magic is everywhere and it can be used to do absolutely anything. Since the beginning of recorded history, we have manipulated our environment with spells and prayers. Belief is the main key to making not only the rituals you will find in this book work, but to making all magic work. If you but believe that you will succeed, you will succeed. It is as simple as that.

May the Love of the Supreme Being be yours.
With love from me to you.

Getting Started

WHEN TO DO A RITUAL

Romantic Spells should always begin when the moon is waxing, the period of time between the New Moon and the Full Moon. This time shines brightly on Rituals and Workings which are intended to Attract, Reunite, Uplift or Improve Situations. Check your calender for the specific dates each month.

The Venus hours are most conducive to love and lovers. Be guided by these planetary hours and arrange your actions and encounters accordingly.

Monday	6:00 am	1:00 and 8:00 pm
Tuesday	3:00 and 10:00 am	5:00 and 12:00 pm
Wednesday	7:00 am	2:00 and 9:00 pm
Thursday	4:00 and 11:00 am	6:00 pm
Friday	1:00 and 8:00 am	3:00 and 11:00 pm
Saturday	5:00 am and Noon	7:00 pm

Specific days are considered more favorable to individuals according to their Signs, and it is natural to do a Ritual or Working on the day which is Astrologically favorable to *you*.

Monday	Capricorn and Leo
Tuesday	Taurus and Cancer
Wednesday	Virgo and Pisces
Thursday	Libra and Aries
Friday	Aquarius and Sagittarius
Saturday	All Signs

Astral Colors for Each Sign

Sign	For those Born between	Astral Colors
Aries	March 21---April 19	Pink and white
Taurus	April 20---May 19	Yellow and red
Gemini	May 20---June 18	Red and blue
Cancer	June 19---July 23	Green and brown
Leo	July 24---August 22	Red and green
Virgo	August 23---September 21	Gold and black
Libra	September 22---October 21	Black and blue
Scorpio	October 22---November 20	Brown and black
Sagittarius	November 21---December 20	Gold and green
Capricorn	December 21---January 19	Red and black
Aquarius	January 20---February 18	Blue and pink
Pisces	February 19---March 20	White and black

Study this list and look at the colors selected for you. Pick the color that suits you best: if you have a favorite color, perhaps it will work better for you. Experiment and change; when you get good results, then continue using that color as your Astral Color.

Candle Burning

You can not have too many candles on hand. So many of my favorite rituals call for candles I keep a huge supply on hand at all times. Once you get the hand of spell-casting, you are certain to be doing the same.

As for which candles you might want to stock, of course, you will decide that for yourself in due time. After all, different candles do different things. Certain colors attune themselves to certain actions. Certain shapes respond better to certain requests.

The rules pertaining to candles are easy to remember. Whatever size or style or color of candle is designated in the spells that follow, use exactly what is called for. Do *not* make substitutions. Also, do *not* use the same candle for more than one ritual. Whereas you should try to use the same tools to make carvings, or the same writing tables, the same bottles to hold your pure water, et cetera, any offerings, candles, oils, et cetera, that you might use, should always be fresh.

—A VERY IMPORTANT NOTE ON CANDLES —

Any candle you plan to use must be cleaned. It does not matter how clean it appears to you. This ritual must be performed with any candle. Certainly you are looking to remove dirt and dust which, if present, *must* be removed. But, we are looking here to remove any negativity that might be present. You have no idea who has handled this candle, the box it was in, the wax which made it, before you did. Because of their waxen nature (wax is an excretion), candles must be cleansed.

To perform this ritual, all you need is an undyed cloth (white with no design or pattern, an old handkerchief, even an old T-shirt) and some alcohol. Soak the cloth, cleanse the candle. You are done and the candle is ready for use.

Also: it is important to note that any candle can only be used for one ritual. Do not reuse any candles—ever! Even if a candle ritual is stopped in the middle, do not use the candle from the ritual later on for anything (except, as noted earlier, to continue that same ritual), even simply for light!

You never know what you can set into motion. Whenever a ritual is over, all candles must be disposed of as soon as possible. Do not worry if someone goes through your trash and takes the candles and burns them. Once you have shown the gods your intention by disposing of the candles, that will be the end of things.

IMAGE CANDLE SPELL
TO WIN SOMEONE'S LOVE

On a Friday as the Moon waxes....

1. Carve your name into an image candle representative of your gender and carve the name of the one you desire on an image candle representative of his/her gender.

2. Anoint both candles with Venus Oil.

3. Mix the following ingredients together as an incense to burn on charcoal: Frankincense, Lavender, Rosemary, Verbena and Anise Seed.

4. Place the image candles to face each other about two inches apart. Light them along with some of the incense mixture.

5. As the candles burn for an hour each day thereafter vision yourself winning the love of your intended a being always together.

6. Repeat each day until the candles are gone, and your lover is under your power of fascination. Bury the wax and ashes in the earth.

> *If you desire, this ritual may be repeated over and over for up to two weeks, using new candles and replenishing your supply of herbs.*

ATTRACT THE LOVE
OF THE OPPOSITE SEX

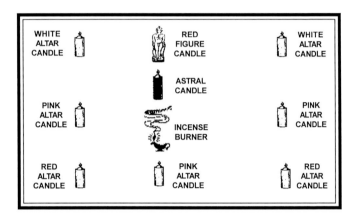

Materials:

Astral Candle - Your astrological color
Red Figure Candle of the opposite sex
Two White Altar Candles
Three Pink Altar Candles
Two Red Altar Candles
Incense Burner
Attraction Incense
Attraction Oil

Procedure:

1. Arrange your altar as shown above.

2. Anoint the red and pink Altar Candles with Attraction oil.

3. Carve into the two Altar Candles the name of the person you wish to attract to you.

4. Light the white Altar Candles.

5. Light the Astral Candle.

6. Light the Attraction Incense.

7. Light the pink Altar Candles, thinking of yourself.

8. Light the red Altar Candles, thinking of the person you wish to be attracted to you.

9. Light the red Figure Candle, thinking of the person you wish to be attracted to you.

10. After lighting all the candles, chant three times the following:

> *Energy* of *Earth, Heat* of *Fire,*
> *Drops of Water, Breath of Air,*
> *May the flames of my candles reach you*
> *And bring you to me.*
> *So Mote It Be!*

Meditate and "think positive" for your desire.
Allow 15 to 30 minutes for the ritual.

TO BRING A LOVER

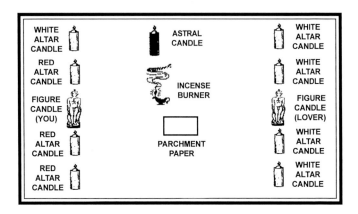

Materials:

One Astral Candles *(Your astrological color)*
2 White Altar Candles *(Stick Candles or Crucifix Candles)*
2 Red Figure Candles *(Your sex and the sex of your desire)*
3 Red Stick Candles
3 Pink Stick Candles
Parchment Paper
Dove's Blood Ink
Quill Pen
Come to Me Incense
Come to Me Oil

Procedure:

1. Anoint the red and pink Altar Candles with Come to Me Oil.

2. Carve the name of your desired lover into the appropriate figure candle.

3. Carve your name into the figure candle that represents you.

4. Write on the Parchment Paper your name and the name of the person you desire, using Dove's Blood Ink.

5. Light the white Altar Candles.

6. Light the Come to Me Incense.

7. Light the red Altar Candles.

8. Light the pink Altar Candles.

9. Light the Figure Candles and Astral Candle.

10. Chant the following six times:

Bring my desired one to be with me.
(Lover's Name) come to me,
So Mote It Be!

Allow three days for this ritual, each day move the
Figure candles closer, to each other, until they touch.

Each day allow 30 minutes for this ritual.
Concentrate diligently on your wish, visualize that it is reality!

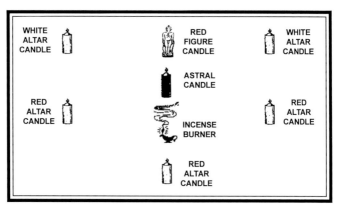

Materials:
• Astral Candle - Your astrological color
• Love Incense
• Red Figure Candle of the opposite sex
• Love Oil
• Two white Altar Candles
• Three red Altar Candles

Procedure:
1. Anoint the red Altar Candles with Love Oil.
2. Light the incense.
3. Light the white Altar Candles.
4. Light the Astral Candle, thinking of yourself
5. Light the red Figure Candle, thinking of your lover.
6. Light the red Altar Candles, thinking of your lover.
7. Chant the following two times:

Love of Mine, the one I love
Stay with me for you are mine
So Mote it be!
Meditate and "think positive" for your desire.
Allow 15 to 30 minutes for the ritual.

SPELL KIT TO
KEEP A LOVER LOYAL

Materials:

1 square of parchment
1 pink candle
1 bottle of Lotus Oil
1 packet Love Drawing Incense

Procedure:

1. Begin this ritual on a Friday night as the moon waxes.

2. Write your lover's name on a piece of parchment.

3. Anoint the pink candle with the Lotus Oil and vision your lover remaining loyal and faithful to you. Stand the candle on the parchment square.

4. Mix a few drops of the oil into the incense. Burn the candle and the mixture.

5. Concentrate on your lover and chant over and over as the candle burns:

LOVER, LOVER, REMAIN BY MY SIDE.
LOVER, LOVER, THY FEELINGS DON'T HIDE.
KEEP THYSELF EVER TO ME.
I SHALL THINE ONLY BE.

Repeat this spell
as often as necessary to accomplish your goal.

THE TRIANGLE OF PASSION SPELL KIT

Materials:

- 3 twigs or sticks 8 inches long
- 2 strips of parchment paper
- 1 red taper candle about 8 inches long
- 1 bottle of Power Oil
- 1 packet of Love Incense

Procedure:

1. On a Friday as the Moon waxes, arrange the three twigs end to end to form a triangle.

2. Write the full name of your lover on one of the strips of parchment. Write your own on the other.

3. Arrange the strips to form a cross in the center of the triangle.

4. Anoint the red candle with the oil as you envision your Lover and yourself in passionate embrace. Stroke the candle with the oil and infuse that idea into it for 5 full minutes.

5. Set the candle to stand in the center of the triangle and light it along with the incense. Chant:

> *EROTIC THOUGHTS OF ME AND THEE*
> *IN THE CANDLE FLAME I SEE _____,*
> *THOU AND I IN LOVE'S PURE LIGHT,*
> *BE THESE THOUGHTS I NOW IGNITE.*

6. Allow the candle to burn for one hour each night as you envision your affair as you would like it to be.

7. On the third night, burn the parchments in the flame and let the candle to burn all the way. Bury the remains.

OLD NEW ORLEANS STYLE LOVE SPELL
SHOULD YOUR LOVER SEEM TO DRIFT AWAY

Materials:

- 7 pink candles
- 7 pieces of parchment paper
- 1 bottle of Cleopatra Oil
- Love Drawing Powder
- Doves Blood Ink

Procedure:

1. Perform this ritual on a Friday night as the moon is waxing.

2. Write your lover's name on each of the pieces of parchment using the Dove's Blood ink.

3. Set the parchments around to form a circle of seven.

4. Anoint each candle with the oil and place one on each piece of parchment.

5. You should then surround the circle of candles with a sprinkling of the powder.

6. Light one candle and concentrate on your Lover being more firmly disposed to you, as the candle burns own, chant over and over:

> *LOVER, LOVER, I CALL TO THEE.*
> *LOVER, THY FACE IN THE FLAME I SEE.*
> *THOU CANST NAUGHT BUT THINK OF ME!*
> *NOTHING DRAWETH BUT ME AND THEE*

7. Burn one candle each night for seven nights there after. You should bury the spent wax and parchments outside by your front door.

8. According to the old tradition, your Lover should return shortly to your side.

SPELL KIT TO
START A FLAME IN ANOTHER'S HEART

During an auspicious waxing Moon
on a Friday night gather these ingredients:

- 1 bottle of Fire Of Love Oil
- 1 Red Jumbo Candle
- Blessed Love Seal

1. Scribe your name and your Lover's name on the reverse of the Blessed Love Seal. This seal is from the book which is sometimes called *"Moses' Magical SpiritArt"*. The seals contained in this book are believed to have many magnificent powers. According to tradition they were taken from ancient Hebrew Holy books and have been passed down through the ages until today when thousands carry them with faith in their effectiveness to bring results by magical means. This particular image is believed to be of great power, it is used by those who wish for assurance of being much loved. It is used to gain and hold the affections of another.

2. Anoint the candle with the oil and place it to stand on top of the Seal.

3. Light the candle and chant out loud:

   BURN, FLAME, LIGHT THIS LOVE, BRIGHT AS THE STARS ABOVE.
   CAUSE HIS/HER HEART TO BEAT FOR ME.
   LIGHT HIS LOVE FOR ALL TO SEE.

4. Allow the candle to burn for 10 minutes and then snuff it out. Repeat the chant three more times. Do the same each day thereafter, until the candle be gone.

SEPARATION KIT TO ATTRACT A LOVER AWAY FROM "THIRD PERSON"

Materials:

- 1 bottle Luv Luv Oil.
- 2 Red Jumbo Candles
- 3 pieces parchment
- 1 White Jumbo Candle

Procedure:

1. As the moon wanes on a Tuesday night, write your name on one parchment, your Lover's name on the second and the Rival's name on the third.

2. Anoint one red Jumbo to be your Lover, in the mind, with the oil and the white Jumbo to be yourself also anointed with the oil.

3. Do not anoint the second red Jumbo which represents the "Third Person".

4. Set your Lover's candle on his/her parchment and the Rival's on that parchment side by side. Set your own candle and parchment about 12 inches away.

5. Light all 3 candles to burn 15 minutes each day as you envision your Lover being drawn more to you away from the Rival.

6. Each day move the two red Jumbos further apart, bringing your Lover's candle closer to your own. After the seventh day, allow them all to burn out. Bury the Rival's stub wax far away from your home. Keep the wax stubs from your lover's candle and yours together as a drawing charm.

TO BE ON YOUR LOVER'S MIND

Materials:

- 1 Jumbo candle of pink
- 1 bottle of Rose Oil

Procedure:

Perform this ritual on a Friday night during a waxing moon, while your lover sleeps.

1. Conjure the vision of your Lover to your mind's inner eye as you anoint the candle with the oil for about a full fifteen minutes.

2. Allow the candle to burn for about hour as you chant:

3. Stare deeply into the flame as you chant his/her name over and over again.

   If you are able to picture his/her face in the flame, the tradition says, thoughts of you will be in lover's dreams.

   Repeat each night until the candle is gone.

SPELL KIT TO
KEEP THY LOVER TRUE
"YOUNG WOMAN'S FANCY"

Materials:

- 1 bottle of Love Oil.
- 1 bottle of Controlling Oil.
- 1 red image candle.
- 1 packet Love incense.
- 1 square of parchment.

Procedure:

1. On a Friday night during a waxing moon, write your name and your Lover's name on the parchment square.

2. Anoint the candle with a mixture of the two oils as you deeply concentrate on your Lover keeping true to you.

3. Set the candle to stand upon the parchment.

4. After Sunset, at Moonrise, light both the candle and the incense to burn for 10 minutes as you chant out loud:

> *LOVER, BE TRUE, LOVER BE MINE.*
> *LOVER BE ENTHRALLED BY ME LOVE SO FINE.*
> *BOUND TO ME, FOREVER TO BE*
> *I BE THE ONLY LOVE FOR THEE.*

Repeat each night until the image candle is gone.

SPELL KIT TO
DRAW BACK A LOVER WHO HAS GONE

Begin on a Saturday night during a waxing moon.

Materials:

- 1 Orange candle if Lover male, or Pink or Red if female.
- 1 bottle of Pine Oil
- 1 square of parchment
- Dove Blood Ink

Procedure:

1. Write the name of your wandering Lover on the parchment.

2. Anoint the candle with the oil as you envision him/her returning to thee. Stroke the candle intently for 15 full minutes seeing in your mind your Lover returning and being bound to you.

3. Place the candle upon the parchment, light it and say:

LET THIS LIGHT SEE ("Lover").
BRING HIM/HER TO ME.
BOUND TO ME FOREVER AND A DAY!

4. Burn the candle each day at Sunset for 15 minutes meditating on the same idea.

Be very sure this is what you truly want and that it makes you happy. It is difficult to undo.

SPELL KIT TO
ATTRACT A LOVER

Materials:

- 1 Red cloth image doll
- 1 bottle Luv Luv Oil
- 1 packet French Love Powder
- 1 packet Love Incense
- 1 packet Compelling Incense
- 1 square of parchment
- 1 bottle Dove Blood Ink

Procedure:

1. Begin this spell on a Friday night under a waxing moon.

2. Using ink on the parchment paper, write a description of the kind of lover you wish to attract.

3. Sprinkle the doll with both the oil and the powder. Pin the parchment on the back head of the doll.

4. Mix equal amounts of the two incenses and burn them as you recite Psalms 45 & 46 from your Bible or Book of Psalms.

5. Wrap the doll in a red cloth and lovingly put it away out of sight.

6. Each night thereafter, bring the doll out, burn some incense and repeat the Psalms until your right lover appears in your life.

SPELL KIT TO
BRING A PROPOSAL OF MARRIAGE

Materials:

- 2 image candles.
- Doves Blood Ink.
- 1 square of parchment 6x6.
- 1 red flannel bag.
- 1 bottle Love Oil.
- 1 packet Love Incense.

Procedure:

1. Draw a circle on the parchment square. Inside, write your name. Outside, around the circle, write the name of the one you desire.

2. Anoint the two candles with the oil and set them face to face in the circle on the parchment paper.

3. Light both candles along with some of the incense.

4. When the candles have melted to stubs, press some of the wax from each candle together and insert the wax, the parchment and 7 pinches of the incense into the flannel bag. Seal it shut.

5. Anoint the bag with the oil and say:

> *LOVER, LOVER, COME TO ME,*
> *BY MY SIDE FOREVER MORE.*
> *LOVER, LOVER, MARRY ME,*
> *THEE I DO ADORE.*

Keep the bag under your pillow, anoint it weekly with the oil and repeat the words.

MAGNETIC LOVE DRAWING CHARM

Materials:

- 1 small Magnet
- 1 Red Lodestone
- 1 Nutmeg of India
- 1 Seal of GoodFortune
- 1 Love Drawing Oil
- 1 Love Drawing Powder
- 1 Red flannel bag

Procedure:

1. On a Friday night, under a waxing moon, write your wish on the back of the Seal of Good Fortune. This seal is from the book which is sometimes called "Moses' Magical Spirit Art". The seals contained in this book are believed to have many magnificent powers. According to tradition they were taken from ancient Hebrew Holy books and have been passed down through the ages until today when thousands carry them with faith in their effectiveness to bring results by magical means. The Seal of Good Fortune also known as The Seal of Spiritual Assistance is designed to bring magical assistance to one's wishes, desires, needs, or requests.

2. Place the Seal, the Magnet, the Lodestone and Nutmeg into the bag and sew it tightly shut with white thread. From that point on, never allow anyone else to touch it.

3. Whenever you are with your intended lover, place 7 drops of the Love Drawng Oil onto the bag and carry it on yourself. All other times, you must keep the bag under your pillow.

4. When you are with your intended lover, dust your fingertips with some Love Drawing Powder.

15 DAY LOVE RITUAL

Begin this spell on a Monday or Friday as the moon waxes.
You must, however, continue for the next 15 days.

Materials:

- 1 bottle of Special Oil # 20.
- 1 bottle of Van Van Oil
- 7 squares of parchment, 2x2.
- 1 container Come To Me Powder
- 7 pink taper candles

Procedure:

1. Write the name of your intended lover on each piece of
   parchment paper. Set the pink candles in a line on each piece of
   parchment.

2. Follow this morning ritual for the next 15 days.

3. Add a few drops of the Van Van Oil in your bath each morning.
   After, dust yourself with a light coating of the Come To Me
   Powder. Then, sprinkle your fresh clothes with a few drops of the
   Special Oil #20.

4. Light the pink candles left to right. Allow them to burn for 15
   minutes as you pray or meditate on drawing your lover to yourself. Repeat this each morning for 15 mornings. Bury the wax
   stubs and parchments near your front door.

POWERFUL CHARMS TO
CONTROL A ROVING LOVER

Materials:

- 7 Red mojo or charm bags
- 7 small squares of parchment
- 7 hairs from your body
- 1 oz. each of these Herbs:
    Lavender, Witch's Grass, Wood Betony, Violet Leaves
- 1 bottle of Flame of Love Oil
- 1 Attraction Powder
- 1 Doves Blood Ink

Procedure:

1. Wait for a Tuesday under a waxing moon.

2. Write your lover's name on each piece of parchment.

3. Place 1 parchment in each red bag.

4. Mix all the herbs together and fill each bag.

5. Place a hair in each bag. Tightly sew the bags with red thread.

6. Dab a drop of the oil on each bag and place one in each corner of your bedroom, under your bed, under your mattress, and one in your pillow case.

7. After, wear the oil and a bit of the powder when you are with and around your lover.

A POTION TO
EXCITE ANOTHER'S AFFECTIONS

Use this potion during a waxing moon on a Friday night at Sunset. This potion is said to sweeten your lover's disposition to you.

1. In a saucepan over the stove, mix a teaspoon each of these herbs: Rosemary, Anise Seed Cloves, Orange Rind, a pinch of ground Cumin, 3 dried Rose Buds.

2. Add Honey and ground Cumin.

3. Bring all to a rapid boil as you gently stir.

4. Simmer slowly and count to 100.

5. Remove from the heat and allow to cool before you strain the liquid.

6. Return to the heat. When you perceive sweet vapors filling your kitchen, pour your potion into cups and serve to the one whose affections you want to excite.

BIND YOUR LOVER TO YOU

Materials:

• 1 bottle of Come To Me Oil
• 1 small Magnet
• 2 Lodestones, 1 Red, 1 Green
• 1 Red flannel bag
• 1 bottle Doves Blood Ink
• 1 photo, or other likeness of your Lover

Procedure:

1. On a Friday night during a waning Moon write both your name and that of your Lover on the back of the photo. Draw three complete circles around the two names.

2. You should then insert the photo, the magnet, the lodestones and a tuft of hair from your head into the bag and seal it tightly shut.

3. Anoint it each Friday thereafter with 7 drops of the oil and keep it safely hid under your mattress.

Seals

A Seal is a magical incantation inscribed on a sheet of Parchment Paper which stands for or suggests a specific reason or purpose.

It is a magical tool which will (only if you copy the Seal yourself) bring to you whatever the Seal represents. Your state of mind is the most important magical power of all. Positive thinking will ensure the success of your wish. It is very important that you consercrate the seal once you have created it. Write the names and birthdates of the two people to be brought together. Include a short statement of your objective. Place the seal between the palms of your hands and state your intention out loud. Create a vivid image in your mind of your desire becoming reality. Concentrate intensely, feel your energy empower the seal. When you can no longer hold this image in your mind, you have completed the process. This seal should be kept protected at all times. Do not allow anyone else to handle it or have knowledge of it.

LOVE SEAL OF VENUS
Relates to affairs of the heart

1. Copy this Seal with Dove's Blood Ink on a piece of Parchment Paper.

2. Put the Seal in a small Red Bag.

3. Anoint the bag with Venus Oil.

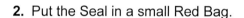

4. Keep the bag with you for seven days. After the seventh day, remove the Seal from the bag.

5. Write on the back of the Seal the name of the person you wish to love you.

6. Anoint a Pink candle with Love Oil.

7. Place the Seal under the Pink candle and light the candle.

8. Let some of the pink wax fall on the Parchment Paper.

9. Burn the Pink candle completely down.

10. Return the Seal to the Red bag.

11. Carry the bag with you for fourteen days. Think positively about your desire.

12. After fourteen days, place the bag in a secure place for safe keeping.

SECOND LOVE SEAL OF VENUS

This Seal is to help you learn the secrets of Love

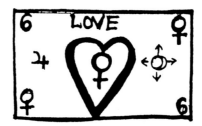

1. Copy this Seal onto a piece of Parchment Paper using Dove's Blood Ink.

2. While copying the Seal, burn a Red candle, and at the same time, burn Love Incense.

3. Anoint the Seal with Love Oil.

4. Pour some of the Red wax from the burning candle onto the Seal.

5. Put the Seal into a Red bag.

6. Keep the bag under your mattress for seven days. Think positively about your desire.

7. After the seven days, keep the Conjure Bag in a safe place.

THIRD LOVE SEAL OF VENUS
This Seal brings the person you love back to you

1. Copy this Seal with Dove's Blood Ink on a piece of Parchment Paper.

2. On the back of the Seal write the person's name that you wish to have come back to you. Write in Dove's Blood Ink

3. Anoint the Seal with Come To Me Oil.

4. Place the Seal in an incense burner.

5. Place Come To Me Incense in the incense burner with the Seal.

6. Light the incense so that the Seal burns as well.

7. Place the ashes in a Red bag and place under your pillow for fourteen days. Think positively about your desire.

8. After fourteen days, place the Red bag in a safe place.

VOODOO VEVE
Seal For Love Drawing

Materials:

- 1 piece of Parchment
- 2 Red lodestones
- 1 bottle Sweet Pea Oil
- 1 Red mojo bag
- Doves Blood Ink

Procedure:

Make this on a Friday as the Moon waxes.

1. Draw the following Seal in the ink on the parchment. Write your name along each side.

2. Anoint the heart with a dab of the Sweet Pea Oil.

3. Place the lodestones and the parchment into the red bag.

4. Seal it tight. Anoint the bag each Friday with a dab of the oil. Carry it always to draw love to yourself.

(NAME)

Herbal Charms For Love

The magical powers of herbal charms come from your state of mind while preparing the charm. You must, while making the charm, think of the purpose you wish to be fulfilled.

Herbal charms are usually handmade and should be kept in a Conjure Bag on the person at all times (unless otherwise indicated in the specific instructions).

Adam & Eve Root - Will bring the one you love closer. Anoint the root with Adam And Eve Oil. Place the root in a Red Conjure Bag and carry it with you.

Archangel - Brings a loved one back. Crush this herb and place it in an incense burner, along with some Come To Me Incense. Burn the root and the incense together. Chant the name of the person you wish to come back.

Coriander - This herb will help you prevent your mate from wandering. Place the herb under your mate's pillow.

Cubeb Berries - Will melt the heart of the one you love. Place in a Red Conjure Bag and keep with you when you talk to your soulmate.

Devil's Shoestring - To bring home a lover wrap some of the root in Pink silk and place under your pillow.

Dragon's Blood Reed - Brings a loved one home. Write on a piece of Parchment Paper the name of your lover in Dove's Blood Ink. Wrap a piece of the Reed in the Parchment Paper. Place the Reed and the Parchment in an incense burner, and burn them.

Guinea Red Pepper - Keep your mate from leaving you. Place two pieces of the Pepper under your mattress.

High John The Conqueror - To win the love of a member of the opposite sex, place the root in a red Conjure Bag which has been anointed with Attraction Oil. Keep with you always.

Lavender - Keeps your lover faithful. Place the herb in a small Pink Conjure Bag and place under your lover's mattress.

Magnolia - Keeps peace between husband and wife. Sprinkle some of the herb or oil under your mattress.

Myrrh - Will bring the one you love closer. Place the Myrrh in an incense burner with some Love Incense and burn.

Orris Root - Attracts members of the opposite sex. Anoint the Orris Root with Attraction Oil and place it in a Pink Conjure Bag. Carry with you at all times.

Rosebuds - Attract a particular member of the opposite sex. Place some Rosebuds in a Red Conjure Bag and place in your bath water.

Scullcap - Keeps your mate faithful. Carry in a Red Conjure Bag.

Tonka Beans - Will keep you and your mate faithful to one another. Place two Tonka Beans in two Red Conjure Bags; one for you and one for your mate. Anoint the bags with Attraction Oil. Place the bags together in a safe place.

Oils for Love

Oils have been used since early times for magical practices, and are still used by many religions even today. The use of these Magical Oils is a fast way to get in touch with the supernatural, and an equally fast way of using odors as a psychological stimulant.

Any of the following oils for love can be used at any time. You may wear the oil as a perfume or as indicated in the Rituals, Seals or Charms. When wearing the oils, the Love Vibrations are enhanced. Refer to the following instructions in preparing and using your love oils to insure best results.

ANOINTING THE BODY

When applying Oils to the body, you must remember the imaginary Magical Triangle that you must work with. You must always start at the base, and work upward to the apex or top. Each side must be stroked upward, firmly, and withan abundance of the Oil. As this is done, the *Power Thought* and concentration on the objective must be utilized.

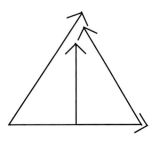

ANOINTING CANDLES

For the best results, you must dress the candle yourself. You are then putting *your* "Vibrations" on the candle, and this makes your work stronger. As you apply the Oil, you must concentrate on the purpose of the Ritual. This *magnetizes* the candle for you.

For the best results, the *"Magic Triangle"* approach should be used. Start at the base and work upwards, one side at a time. This Magical Triangle is the oldest way of Dressing a candle, and has been used extensively by Witches for thousands of years.

ANOINTING A SEAL

Anointing a Seal makes it stronger as a Magical Tool. When applying the Oil, you must concentrate on the purpose of the Seal, and its intended use. The correct procedure for applying the Oil is to wet the finger tip with the Oil, apply the Oil to each corner, starting with the upper left one, and then working clockwise, do the rest of the corners. The second step is to then trace an imaginary line, starting with the same corner and proceeding clockwise around the edge of the Seal until you come back to the starting corner. This *closes in* the Power of the Seal, and makes it very effective.

The anointing should be done on a weekly basis to maintain the Power of tile Seal.

ANOINTING A MOJO OR CHARM

You must use the appropriate Oil to *Magnetize* an Amulet, Charm or Mojo. The Oil is applied in the bag while being made, or on the outer edges of a Talisman, Amulet or Charm. In addition, the object must be held by the maker to put the necessary Power and magnetism into it with the thought and concentration on the purpose.

Adam and Eve Oil - Anoint the body to bring your lover to you. Have some on your hand when seeing your intended; put some on him/her and he/she will be yours from then on.

Attraction Oil - Anoint pink candles to bring him/her to you. If anointed on a Charm or Amulet, it will bring someone new to you. Brings your lover back when placed on a red candle.

Cleopatra Oil - Used by lovers to increase sexual enjoyment; anoint the bodies and the bed sheets. To bring back a drifting lover, anoint seven red candles made of beeswax. Place them in a circle, and burn one each night at midnight.

Come To Me Oil - Anoint the breasts to entice love. When a Red Astral Candle is anointed, you can draw the one you want to come to you.

Fast Love Oil - Will bring him or her to you rapidly. Anoint his/her clothing or shoes. Put some on your hand, rub it on him or her.

Glow of Attraction Oil - A strong Attraction Oil. Place behind the ears, and attract new lovers to you.

Heart Oil - Strengthens the Power of the heart's desire, and gets you what you want. You must anoint the heart area everyday.

Isis Oil - Anoint the forehead, and call the old Goddess of Love to assist you. Gain the attributes of the Goddess by using this oil in your bath daily. A sexually stimulating perfume brings on unexpected prowess and sexual pleasures.

Lodestone Oil - Draws good luck in all matters. Anoint love charms, seals, bags, candles, roots and spells with this oil to help draw love.

Love Oil - Anoint the body and draw him or her to you. If both are anointed over the heart, the love will be eternal.

Love Bait Oil - Used to entice a man into a relationship. Wear the Oil on the wrists, and you will draw him in.

Love Bath Oil - Mix into bath water, and love will come to you.

Love Drops Oil - Apply to the sexual areas, and your lover will always want to be with you.

Love's Fires Oil - Used to generate an interest by another. Mix into Incense, and burn in his/her presence. Wear it and carry it as an Oil.

Luv Luv Oil - To bring someone to you as a new lover, away from someone else. Must be put on a Mojo or Conjure Bag, and worn.

Marriage Oil - Rub this oil on the hair of your lover, and then he will want to marry you.

Passion Oil - Apply to the arms and legs. This will arouse the passion and the love that you want. Can also be added to bath water.

Rose Oil - A Love Oil to bring him to you and keep him.

Salome - Used to tease a man, and then bring him to you. Wear on the clothing, and be in his presence.

San Cipriano - Anoint the ears to bring back a wandering husband.

7-Knot Love Oil - Tie seven knots on a cord and anoint each knot with this love oil once each week. Focus on your intended and carry this with you at all times until your love comes.

Violet Oil - Violet oil is attributed to the Goddess of Love. Wear this Oil and be modest and then things will come to you.

Wild Desire Oil - A strong oil to get what you desire. Wear the oil on the hair each day, and receive your strongest wants.

Working with the Psalms

The following pages contain a variety of uses to which the psalms have been applied. By saying the particular psalm over and over with an intent, a specific purpose may be achieved.

When utilizing the psalms to achieve your goals it is vital that your purpose is stated specifically both before and after reading the psalm aloud.

PSALM #3

BREAK UP A LOVE AFFAIR - On a Saturday, light a Black candle and pray this psalm along with the following affirmation out loud, three times each, as the candle burns.

> *"Here is one half of the pair,*
> *Now his (her) love nest will soon be single*
> *And the Gold in my heart will jangle jingle.*
> *For what seems plain now seems plain*
> *And what was Sunshine has now turn to rain."*

PSALM #11

BRING A LOVED ONE TO YOU - Burn a Red candle with the name of your loved one written on it. Repeat the psalm 9 times as the candle burns and the loved one will respond.

PSALM #20

BRING BACK A HUSBAND - Scratch his name on a Red male figure candle, anoint it with Come to Me Oil. As the candle burns, read the psalm and ask that he be returned. Do this every other night for the period of a month. Read the psalm with strength and the divine force will be with you.

PSALM #31

GAIN A LOVER - Read this psalm while burning a Red candle and wish for the love whom you desire. The love and affection you desire will be yours.

PSALM #37

KEEP A SPOUSE OR LOVER FAITHFUL - Write this psalm on a piece of parchment paper. Wet the paper with Glory Water, then hide it where no one else can find it. Add one bottle of Love Drawing Oil to your bath for 7 days in a row. Use Strong Love Cologne whenever you are in the presence of your loved one.

PSALM #65

BE LUCKY IN LOVE AFFAIRS - Use Lover's Oil on your arms and neck. Read this psalm before going out to meet the one of your dreams. Suggest taking a bath or shower together and pour some of the oil over each of you.

PSALM #45 and #46

Psalms 45 and 46 are said to possess the virtue of making peace between a man and wife.

TO TAME AN ILL-TEMPERED WIFE - To make an irritable spouse more friendly and loveable a man should pronounce the 45th Psalm over Olive Oil, and anoint himself with it. Differences can be further renconciled by anointing the woman with the Olive Oil as well.

MAKE A HUSBAND LOVE HIS WIFE - A woman should burn a Red candle and and Lovers Incense, say the psalm several times while standing in the bedroom. Write the psalm on parchment paper and place the paper under his side of the bed.

PSALM #67

ATTRACT A LOVER - Pray Psalm 67 each morning when you rise. Place 7 drops of Venus Oil in your morning bath. When you dress to leave the house, sprinkle your clothing with Attraction Powder.

KEEP A MARRIAGE STRONG - Pray Psalm 67 with your partner frequently to keep your marriage or relationship solid. Burn a Pink Candle anointed with Lovers Oil and your relationship will stay strong. and passionate.

PSALM #85

REPAIR A BROKEN LOVE AFFAIR - On a Friday, light a Blue candle and pray this psalm along with the following affirmation out loud as the candle burns.

"Our love is not a sometimes thing, our love is like a diamond ring.
No anger do I hold toward you, no doubt do I possess.
So you now come back and always know,
That it's YOU I love the best!"

PSALM #88

REGAIN A LOVER - Burn a Red figure candle anointed with Come To Me Oil, as you read this psalm and call on your lover to return. Continue to alternate between the reading and the call as the candle burns.

MAKE SOMEONE CALL YOU - Place some Mistletoe under the telephone and then read the psalm over the telephone. Repeat this each evening until you receive the call you are waiting for.

PSALM #111

LOVE SPELL - Before going out to a party or other social occasion, read this psalm in its entirety by the light of a Pink Candle. Wear some Florida Water or any other essence that includes Cinnamon and Orange Blossom as an ingredient. You will meet someone specoal that day.

PSALM #138

ATTRACT LOVE - If you are a man begin his ritual on a Friday and burn a blue candle, if you are a woman begin this ritual on a Tuesday and burn a Yellow candle. Repeat this affirmation and psalm aloud seven times while the candle burns. Be sure that you have engraved the initials of your desired mate on the candle.

"It's me you love, I know it's true"
"It's me you love, You know it too!"

ITEM #172
$9.95

HELPING YOURSELF WITH
MAGICKAL OILS A-Z

By Maria Solomon

**The most thorough and comprehensive
workbook available on the**

Magickal Powers of
Over 1000 Oils!

**Easy to follow step-by-step instructions
*for more than 1500
Spells, Recipes and Rituals for*
Love, Money, Luck, Protection
and much more!

ISBN 0-942272-49-8 5½" x 8½" $9.95

ITEM #224
$6.95

Revised and Expanded

Success and Power Through Psalms

By Donna Rose

For thousands of years, men and women have found in the Psalms the perfect prayer book, possessing wisdom applicable to every human situation. Wise men and women of deep mystical insight have also learned to decipher the magical formulas David and the other Psalmists hid behind the written words. These formulas help the seeker solve everyday problems, achieve higher states of consciousness, gain material and spiritual wealth, as well as help defend himself or herself against psychic attacks and all manner of dangers.

The Revised and Expanded edition of Donna Rose's classic offers over 300 simple to perform magical rituals to help you manifest all of your desires using the magical powers of the psalms.

ISBN 0-942272-79-X 5½"x 8½ $6.95